MINI-GUIDES

SOLDIERS IN NORMANDY: THE BRITISH.........

June to August 1944

by Alexandre THERS

Lay-out by the author and Yann-Erwin ROBERT

Translated from the French by Jonathan NORTH

h&c
PARIS

BRITISH COMBAT CAPABILITY IN NORMANDY

Although 850,000 British, Canadian and Polish soldiers took part in the Normandy campaign they were outnumbered by the 1,200,000 Americans who formed the rest of the invading armies. Even so, with 3,300 medium tanks as opposed to the 2,000 fielded by the Americans, they contributed the most imposing armored force. What was the morale of the soldiers, how were they organized and what was their combat value?

Qualities and Faults

Great Britain was traditionally a maritime power and was slow to develop its land forces. The rapid development of the air force further contributed to the disparity. So it was that after 1942, when losses were taken into account, it was found that there weren't sufficient Army replacements in reserve. Despite contributions from the colonies and dominions, Britain lacked manpower. Consequently, only 38,900 men were sent as reinforcements to Normandy for the entire campaign. It was clearly an insufficient number and led to the disbanding, on August 16, 1944 of the 59th Division plus one brigade of the 49th. This was rapidly followed by the disbandment of the 50th Division.

The divisions deployed in Normandy were of two kinds. There were those which had some experience of combat and those which had been newly trained. Of the infantry divisions, only the 50th (Northumberland) and 51st (Highland) had fought in North Africa, Sicily and Italy and they had acquired brilliant reputations. Of the armored divisions only the 7th Armoured Division (the famous Desert Rats) had seen action in North Africa, although the others were fully trained for combat. The green formations would face new and terrible odds in Normandy, while the veteran divisions were sometimes in no condition psychologically to give their all in the new battle. With the exception of the 3rd Infantry Division the other divisions in Normandy were composed of Territorial Army units which had only been elevated to Regular Army status in the middle of 1942. Despite extensive training they fought less well than the average American unit. On the other hand, the best fighting spirit could be found within commando and paratrooper units.

In general British cooperation between infantry and tanks was poor, even within the armored divisions. Infantry was always lacking and even if it was carried in trucks it could rarely keep up the pace of the tanks. Superb morale in some cavalry and infantry units also meant that there was a tendency for some formations to act independently. Overall, infantry and armor were committed separately and piecemeal. The Canadians had better liaison between tanks and infantry and were capable of fashioning flexible combined arms groups, similar to the German concept.

Training

As with his predecessor in the First World War, the British soldier showed legendary tenacity in defense and methodical prudence when on the attack. The training doctrine devised for British troops was less harsh than that in use by the Germans, although battle indoctrination was taught in realistic 'Battle Schools.' But on the eve

4

of D-Day, some British units had spent four years drilling in the British countryside and this lack of purpose had a bad effect on morale and had suppressed the martial spirit of the troops and made them doubt the abilities of their officers. These latter certainly had their work cut out in preparing their men for combat operations. The Canadians, on the other hand, were excellent with good morale and cohesion due, in large measure, to the men being volunteers.

The Organization of British Divisions

A British infantry division had a theoretical strength of 18,347 men but most lacked around 2,000 men and it was rare for a division to even boast 16,000 effectives in the field. The division was based on three brigades of infantry, each of three battalions, supported by the divisional artillery (3 field artillery regiments, one anti-tank and one anti-aircraft regiments) and various service units.

The armored division had a theoretical strength of 14,964 and essentially consisted of an armored brigade of three tank regiments plus a battalion of mechanized infantry in half-tracks. The divisional armored reconnaissance regiment meant that, in effect, there were four tank regiments and allowed for the attachment of a regiment of tanks per infantry battalion. In all there were 244 medium and light tanks 25 anti-aircraft guns and eight command vehicles. The armored divisions and independent armored brigades which fought in Normandy fielded nearly 3,300 Sherman, Churchill and Cromwell tanks. There were eight independent armored brigades and five armored divisions (plus one Polish division) so, unlike the Germans, the majority of tanks were not assigned to divisions. The Polish troops were equipped and trained in an identical manner to their British counterparts.

The Context

One of the essential aspects of the Normandy landings was to ensure the securing of the landing beaches as quickly as possible. This task was assigned to General Percy Hobart's division of special tanks. When actually on the Norman battleground, the British felt the lack of self-propelled anti-tank guns keenly. The time it took to get towed guns into action in such terrain rendered them vulnerable. The supply of armor-piercing shells meant they could only fire on AFVs and were ineffective against infantry. These disadvantages were largely offset by the benefits brought about by omnipresent Allied air superiority and by a powerful field artillery. Due to the quality of their gunners and field pieces, the British could bring to bear overwhelming concentrations of fire at given points. The combined efforts of artillery and tactical aviation neutralized the Panzers and rendered the movement of supplies to the front virtually impossible. All this made the task of the Sherman and Cromwell tanks that much easier.

Losses

The British, Canadians and Poles lost heavily throughout the Normandy campaign. On D-Day some 2,700 British soldiers became casualties as well as 946 Canadians. Of these, some 1,200 of the killed and wounded belonged to airborne troops (not including glider pilots, of whom around 100 were lost). In all 83,045 British, Canadian and Polish soldiers were lost during the Normandy campaign.

THE NAVAL GUNNER

In overall support of the amphibious assault of Normandy, the Royal Navy had 2,468 warships of all types compared with the Americans' 346. Naturally it played a prominent part in the naval operation ('Neptune') which preceded the landings ('Overlord'). Among the larger vessels in action on D-Day were the battleships HMS Ramillies *and HMS* Warspite *which bombarded German positions.*

Other ships involved were the minesweepers, which played a major part in clearing a passage for the invasion fleets in infested waters; landing craft and launches which ferried British and Canadian troops from transports to the beaches; and destroyers, frigates and corvettes which took part in the operation and protected the Allied fleet against submarines and enemy vessels. There were two Monitor-class cruisers

*T*his sailor wears a Duffle Coat as protection against the inclement weather. *(The Bachmann collection)*

*N*avy issue cigarettes in a metal tin. *(The Bachmann collection)*

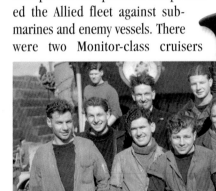

A sailor's jack-knife, with a regular blade and marlin spike. *(Bachmann collection)*

*S*ailors of the sloop Aviso, a British ship which formed part of the armada's escort. Some 10,000 Canadian sailors also participated in Operation Neptune. *(IWM)*

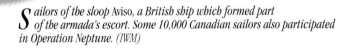

A sailor's blue cap. As the war began having the ship's name on the front was phased out and caps just bore HMS (His Majesty's Ship). *(Bachmann collection)*

*N*aval gunners. These men wear life preservers.
(IWM)

*A*rm badge worn by the signals petty officers.
(Bachmann collection)

involved as well and these gave close fire support to the troops on the beaches as did other cruisers. Finally there were other warships armed to repel air raids. The Royal canadian Navy was also heavily involved in 'Neptune' with 109 warships.

The guns of HMCS *Algonquin* and HMCS *Sioux* reduced German shore batteries to silence and supported troops engaged on the ground. The navy carried out its task of ferrying troops to shore extremely efficiently, winning the admiration of many landlubbers.

After giving its all in this major operation the Royal Navy went on to play a less high-profile role, its principal task being the security of the flow of supplies heading across the Channel and attempts to force open the ports of Belgium and Holland.

*T*his sailor was probably assigned to watch duty. On the chilly morning of June 6 he'd be wearing a knitted Balaclava, a Duffle Coat, long socks and sea boots. (Photo by A. Ward)

THE GLIDER PILOT

Glider pilots had their moment of fame on June 6 when six Horsa gliders, carrying airborne troops, were given the task of securing the bridges on the Orne canal at Bénouville and Ranville.

A glider pilot in Great Britain in June 1944. The Glider Pilot Regiment's motto was "Nihil est Impossibilis" (Nothing is Impossible).

The Glider Pilot Regiment was made up of volunteers trained by the Army Air Corps. Candidates were then assigned to the Regiment as NCOs if they were of sufficient mental and physical ability. In addition to flying in the gliders, they were supposed to fight as infantrymen after the landing. They were therefore trained in infantry fighting and were quite capable of using a number of weapons.

For active operations, Glider pilots were organized into two Wings each of seven squadrons of four flights of gliders and one squadron of transports. The personnel roughly corresponded to a battalion of infantry, although they were less heavily armed. The pilots flew two types of glider.

The Airspeed Horsa, a medium glider of 6.97 tons could carry infantrymen, or an anti-tank gun and a jeep.

A glider pilot's crash helmet. Rubber cups on the sides housed earphones, the microphone for communication with the towing plane was attached to snaps on the sides. (Militaria Magazine)

The General Aircraft Hamilcar, a heavier glider of 16.2 tons had been developed to transport the Tetrarch light tank. The crew of each glider comprized a pilot and a co-pilot. Of the six gliders which tasked with the Orne bridges mission at Bénouville just after midnight on June 6, three, piloted by Staff

This glider pilot has been captured by the Germans. He sports the 'Army Flying Badge' (glider pilot wings) in his chest. (Bundesarchiv)

Left: An electric dynamo lamp. (Militaria Magazine)

Sergeants Jim Wallwork, Oliver Boland and G. Barkway, were spot on target whilst two (piloted by R. Howard and S. Pearson) were about 170 yards off. The sixth, piloted by A. Lawrence, was off course and ended up some ten miles from its intended target. The operation was, however, a resounding success and the airlanded troopers held the bridges until joined by commandos which came by sea on June 6 in the morning.

Later that day some 16 other gliders participated in Operation Mallard designed to reinforce those men of the 6th Airborne Division who had already landed near the bridges.

A British Army wristwatch ('Army Time Piece'). *(Militaria Magazine)*

A Glider Pilot sergeant. He wears the Airborne troops' camouflaged Denison smock, with regular wool Battledress trousers, anklets and black boots. *(Reconstruction by Militaria Magazine)*

9

THE COMMANDO

The commandos were small units of specially trained men, specifically equipped for raids on the enemy coast. They usually acted independently and, on June 6, were the first troops to reach Sword Beach.

The commandos deployed on D-Day belonged to No 3, 4, 6 and 10 (Army) Commandos and No 45 (Royal Marine) Commando, all grouped under the 1st Special Service Brigade, and No 41, 46, 47 and 48 (Royal Marine) Commandos under the 4th Special Service Brigade. No 4 Commando's 8 Troop was made up of Free French commanded by Navy Captain P. Kieffer. The 1st Special Service Brigade landed at Sword in the sector of the 3rd Division and was given the task of taking the Riva-Bella battery. It was then to push towards Caen and join up with elements of the 6th Airborne Division at the Orne River and Caen canal bridges. No 46 and 48 Royal Marine Commandos landed at Juno in the sector of the 3rd Canadian Division and were given the mission of striking out to the west of Caen and pushing eastwards to link up with 41 Commando respectively. This latter junction was to take place at Lion-sur-Mer (Sword). No 47 hit land by Arromanches

ALL-IN FIGHTING

W. E. FAIRBAIRN

*A*bove : a hand-to-hand fighting handbook for Commandos.
(Militaria Magazine)

A British Army commando. He wears the commandos' green beret and carries a heavy rucksack loaded with ammunition. The special fighting knife is strapped to the trouser leg.
(Reconstruction by J. Bouchery/ Militaria Magazine)

These commandos have been photographed near Ouistreham. Street fighting in Langrune-sur-Mer cost No 48 Royal Marine Commando heavy casualties. (IWM)

The formation sign for British Commando ('Combined Operations') units. In 1940 a commando school was established in Scotland and volunteers from Allied countries, including France and the USA, were trained there. (Militaria Magazine)

(Gold Beach) with the 50th Division and headed westwards to Port-en-Bessin. No 3 Commando pushed towards the Orne bridges and took up a position at Amfreville in expectation of a German counter attack. No 4 Commando landed at Ouistreham and, after clearing the landing area, launched an assault against the casino which the Germans had fortified. The French carried the position after heavy losses and also captured the German headquarters at Colleville-sur-Orne before pushing on for Amfreville. At around 20.00 it took up position at Hauger. From then until June 10, Kieffer's men enjoyed a brief lull in the fighting as they assumed a defensive posture. As for No 6 it linked up with the glider borne infantry around the Orne bridges early on in the afternoon. No 46 managed to destroy the German batteries at Houlgate and Bénerville and then launched a diversionary attack towards Cabourg whilst No 41 seized a German defensive position before advancing towards the village of Petit-Enfer (Luc-sur-Mer). Here it met No 48 which had been tasked with neutralizing German coastal defenses around Langrune-sur-Mer. These held out until the following day. Lion-sur-Mer was also liberated and junction was made with No 46 Commando. This latter unit managed to take Petit-Enfer after some particularly brutal hand-to-hand fighting and then moved off to Luc-sur-Mer.

Ouistreham, June 6, 1944. This French sailor, from No 4 Commando, wears combat equipment. (IWM)

Top: A French commando photographed on June 6 near Riva-Bella. He is armed with a K-gun, a drum-fed machinegun with a high rate of fire. (DR)

Right: the Fairbairn-Sykes knife was issued to commandos and paratroopers for hand-to-hand fighting. (DR)

THE PARATROOPER

The 6th Airborne was the only such British division that took an active part in operations on June 6. Its mission was to protect the left flank of I Corps by securing the area between the Orne and the Dives rivers.

Committed along an axis formed by Troarn, Sannerville and Colombelles, the division was to seize two bridges which crossed the Caen Canal to Caen at Bénouville (now 'Pegasus Bridge') and, 600 yards from there, a bridge over the Orne (now 'Horsa Bridge'). It was also supposed to seize the Merville battery which covered all the principal avenues of attack in the Caen region. A British airborne division consisted of two parachute brigades and a brigade of air landing infantry transported by gliders. Its theoretical strength was 12,416 but, because of a significant

Top: This paratrooper is talking to French civilians as he stands guard on a bridge over the Orne (perhaps Horsa Bridge). (IWM)

Inset: British paratrooper wings, worn on the sleeve. (Militaria Magazine)

This paratrooper wears the airborne troops' special uniform: rimless steel helmet, camouflaged Denison Smock, wool trousers with expanding thigh pocket. He is armed with the Bren light machinegun. (Reconstruction by Militaria Magazine)

These paratroopers are a few of the reinforcements flown over by gliders into Normandy soon after June 6. (IWM)

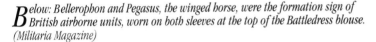

Below: Bellerophon and Pegasus, the winged horse, were the formation sign of British airborne units, worn on both sleeves at the top of the Battledress blouse. (Militaria Magazine)

This glider borne infantryman has the special rimless steel helmet issued to airborne troops, here covered with a net garnished with strips of brown and green hessian for camouflage. (IWM)

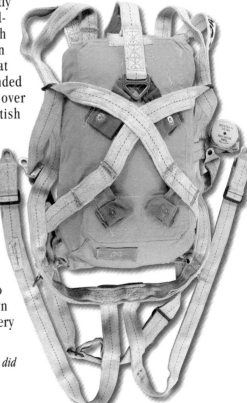

lack of transport, only some 7,500 took part in the initial operation, taking off on June 5. Shortly after midnight the first gliders, belonging to the 5th Brigade, touched down around the Caen canal at Bénouville. One glider landed very close to the bridge over the canal and the British seized the bridge and a German position. Then scouts began marking out a landing zone for the second wave which began to come in not far away at Ranville. This wave reinforced the first and began to prepare the ground for the next wave, marking out landing sites and clearing them of obstacles. Further to the east, along the Dives, the 3rd Brigade missed their drop zone but managed to destroy four bridges over the river.

Meanwhile a the 1st Canadian Parachute battalion destroyed the Varaville Bridge over the Divette and also that at Robehomme. The Troarn bridge was also blown up. Finally, the 9th Para Battalion seized the Merville Battery at 04.45 after an epic fight.

The British type X parachute was deemed so reliable that paratroopers did not enjoy the safety of an emergency chest pack. (Militaria Magazine)

THE SAPPER

The British Royal Engineers were essentially charged with slowing down an enemy advance by creating obstacles or laying mines or, on the contrary, speeding up the progress of their own troops by clearing paths through minefields or repairing bridges.

A Canadian mine clearing team south of Caen, July 1944. Sappers were trained to fight and were used as infantry when the need arose. (Public Archives of Canada)

In addition, however, they also contributed to the effort by constructing supply dumps, air fields, pipelines and so on. They also had more specialist functions: chemical weapons, topography (Survey) and communications. Divisional engineers were composed of a Main HQ, a Field Park (with vehicles) and, for an infantry division three field companies or, for an armored unit, two field squadrons. An airborne division had a field company and two field squadrons. At corps level there were three field companies, a field park and a topographical unit whilst at Army level there were a number of supply units, road construction units, tunnel units

A warning sign for mines. The formation sign at top and code number 62 indicate this was posted by sappers of the Royal Welch Fusiliers (53rd Division) (J. Bouchery collection)

A Canadian engineer gingerly defuses an antitank mine. The Germans had a devilish knack for booby-trapping large mines with hidden devices. (Public Archives of Canada)

The Tellermine 35 was the German Army's standard anti-tank mine up until the end of 1942 when it began to be replaced by the Tellermine 1942. Thousands were placed along coastal defensive positions but were also sown behind as the Nazis retreated to the Seine. (Private collection)

A D8 Caterpillar unloads a locomotive from a transport ship. (IWM)

and vehicle repair workshops. Among the more specialist units we mentioned the chemical weapons unit but there were also assault units supplied with special armored bridging vehicles (AVREs). These were used as an emergency during the assault to cross anti-tank ditches, obstacles or creeks. When crossing rivers, sappers ferried the infantry in inflatable boats and on 'Kapok' footbridges. Inflatable floats and assortment of metal girders were needed for pontoon bridges that could support motor transport. Finally, metal bridging equipment was also employed, from lightweight 'Small Box Girder Bridges' to the ubiquitous Bailey Bridge.

When called upon to perform demolitions, sappers could made use of TNT, dynamite or plastic explosives. The most commonly available mines were the Mk II, Mk IV and Mk V anti-tank mines and the Hawkins 75, Shrapnel and Clam antipersonnel mines.

On June 6, the Royal Engineers deployed a specialist assault brigade in order to demolish beach obstacles.

Top: the Royal Engineers cap badge. Officers were commissioned after three years of training. (Militaria Magazine)

This 'Beach group' sapper has been tasked with clearing beach exits with a Mk III ('Polish') Mine Detector. (Reconstruction by Militaria Magazine)

THE CANADIAN INFANTRYMAN

Two divisions of Canadian infantry fought in Normandy, the 3rd and 2nd. Formed from enthusiastic volunteers, they distinguished themselves on the battlefield. The 3rd, along with the 2nd Canadian Armored Brigade, formed part of the initial assault wave on D-Day.

The 3rd Division landed on Juno Beach between Graye-sur-Mer and Saint-Aubin-sur-Mer. Its objective was to secure the beachhead before pushing inland towards Caen and seizing the airfield at Carpiquet. It also had to link up with troops from Gold Beach in the west and Sword Beach in the east. The Canadians suffered heavy losses when they clashed on June 7, with the 12th SS Panzer-Division ('Hitlerjugend') and the 21st Panzer Division. Their progress towards Caen was checked and it would take a month of bitter fighting before the town fell.

A n infantry company of the 3rd Canadian Division, heads to the front on July 13, 1944. Like all Canadians serving overseas, they are volunteers. (IWM)

A Canadian infantryman, clothed and equipped in a similar manner to his British counterpart. There were a few differences however, notably the greener shade of the wool uniform and yellowish webbing gear.
(Reconstruction by Militaria Magazine)

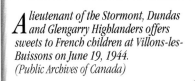

A lieutenant of the Stormont, Dundas and Glengarry Highlanders offers sweets to French children at Villons-les-Buissons on June 19, 1944.
(Public Archives of Canada)

A Canadian corporal during the heavy fighting around Caen in July 1944. He carries a large spade on his back.
(IWM)

The large pack was only worn on the march.
(Militaria Magazine)

Below: The helve and head of the issue entrenching tool. The socket at the end of the handle allows a Mk II bayonet to be fixed there so it could be used as a weapon of last resort in hand-to-hand fighting.
(Militaria Magazine)

On June 9, the Canadians were hit by at least two vicious counter-attacks from the Hitlerjugend around Bretteville. The unit later participated in Operation Epsom, launched to the west of Caen on June 24, again fighting the Hitlerjugend, as well as the battles for the airstrip at Carpiquet in early July. In this fighting the Canadians showed considerable élan but they were forced by the SS to go to ground after having reached the objective. The division then went on to take part in Operation 'Goodwood,' which saw them attack Caen before moving off for Bourguébus and Falaise. The 2nd Canadian Division landed on July 7 and it fought hard for the fortified villages of Saint-André-sur-Orne, Verrières, Saint-Martin-de-Fontenay, Ifs and Bourguébus. It was there, between July 19 and 21, that they were locked in combat with the 1st SS Panzer Corps. Like their comrades in the 3rd Division, the Canadians participated in Operation Totalize in August and suffered heavily. Despite their stubbornness, the operation was not a particular success. Along with the 3rd, the division fought at Falaise and played an important part in closing the pocket.

THE TANKER

Five armored divisions (the 79th, 7th, 11th, the Guards and the 4th Canadian) fought in Normandy, as well as eight independent brigades. The 1st Polish armored division was also committed in the closing stages of the battle. In all, these troops manned 3,300 tanks, a formidable asset to the Allied plan.

One of the British divisions, the 79th was unique in terms of equipment and organization and it played a crucial role on June 6. It was equipped with a number of tank-based armored vehicles, including amphibious tanks, mine-destroying tanks and bridge layers, all designed to secure the beaches. The 79th had no infantry and no artillery component but it fulfilled its support role to perfection. At Gold Beach, for example, a tank armed with a 290-mm mortar destroyed a number of blockhouses and enemy positions.

Once the Allies had secured the beach-head they then had to develop different tactics for the push inland. Tactics were dictated by the terrain but also by the need to seize crossroads and communication hubs to enable Allied armor to deploy effectively and initiate a large-scale battle. The only really practical arena for such a battle was

J uly 1944: the crew of a Churchill tank replenish their MG ammunition. (IWM)

R ight: The 79th Armored Division formation sign. (Militaria Magazine)

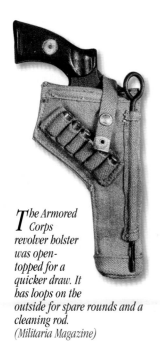

T he Armored Corps revolver holster was open-topped for a quicker draw. It has loops on the outside for spare rounds and a cleaning rod. (Militaria Magazine)

A Sherman tank crew take a break. To offset its 75-mm gun's deficiencies, the British introduced the 'Firefly' variant, armed with the deadly long-barreled 76,2-mm gun, which could destroy most German tanks at long range. (IWM)

ROYAL ARMOURED CORPS

Sherman 'Fireflies' of the Guards Division near the Orne river in July 1944. (IWM)

Inset, top: the Royal Armoured Corps shoulder title, worn on the sleeves. (Militaria Magazine)

The crew of a Sherman III of the 27th Independent Tank Brigade. (IWM)

the plain to the south of Caen. But the British command proved too hesitant and deployed their tanks piecemeal, sometimes overly isolated and without infantry support, and attempted to use them to accomplish short-term objectives usually designed to counter enemy armor. It is therefore not surprising that the Germans usually held the initiative. In addition, British tanks were often outclassed by those of their adversaries and British tank crews suffered heavy losses. The American-made Sherman, for example, which was the backbone of most armored units, could not compete with its German equivalent in terms of armor-plating or gunnery. But, as with the Americans, the British enjoyed a numerical advantage as well as excellent cooperation with tactical aviation.

This tank crewman wears the denim tank suit introduced in 1944. It was worn by itself in warm weather or over the woolen Battledress. The black beret is the armored regiments' trademark. (Reconstruction by J. Bouchery/Militaria Magazine)

THE MOTORCYCLE DISPATCH RIDER

Motorcycles were widely employed throughout the British Army right up to the end of the war. When compared with other types of vehicle they had significant advantages they were small and easily hidden, reliable and were adept at crossing all kinds of terrain.

Motorcycles were relatively cheap to produce and their maintenance was easy. They were used by airborne forces; in recce or liaison units

*T*he sleeve proficiency badge for dispatch riders. *(Militaria Magazine)*

A Military Police corporal belonging to the 15th (Scottish) Division controls traffic over a bridge over the Odon on July 16, 1944. *(IWM)*

*T*he distinctive crash helmet, gloves, laced boots and breeches are typical of dispatch riders. The white and blue arm brassard denotes a Corps of Signals messenger.
(Reconstruction by J. Bouchery/Militaria Magazine)

20

The motorcycle helmet was inspired by that worn by paratroopers and was introduced at the end of 1942. It was used by drivers and passengers.
(Militaria Magazine)

This dispatch rider belongs to a Canadian armored unit in Great Britain. He rides a Norton Model 1G-H.
(CND photo)

This Canadian dispatch rider wears a helmet made of varnished conglomerate of British manufacture. It was worn at the start of the war before the Mk I came into use.
(CND photo)

attached to headquarters; in artillery and infantry units, and by the military police.

They were also used by Royal Air Force personnel, especially by pilots who needed to travel large distances to reach their planes which had been scattered about for security purposes. Female volunteers of the Auxiliary Territorial Service (ATS) also rode such machines in rear-area duties, as well as servicing hundreds of bikes in workshops. Patrols sent out by the Liaison Regiment 'Phantom,' a secret communications or liaison unit, each used two bikes.

Thousands of bikes were landed during the invasion as it was crucial for the high command to find out what was going on through messengers when the radio or telephone failed.

It is noteworth that the thousands of American jeeps given to the Allies under Lend-lease sounded the demise of the motorcycle as a military vehicle in most armies.

A motorcyclist's pair of leather gloves.
(Militaria Magazine)

Goggles used by vehicle drivers, crews and motorcyclists.
(Militaria Magazine)

THE BRITISH INFANTRYMAN

The British deployed three divisions of infantry for the initial assault on the shore. These were the 3rd and 50th divisions and 3rd Canadian division.

T he formation sign of the 43rd (Wessex) Division, a yellow wyvern. (Militaria Magazine)

B elow: Dog tags and an identity bracelet acquired privately. If the wearer of the dog tag was killed the green tag was usually buried with the body. (Militaria Magazine)

The 3rd Division landed on Sword beach on June 6 and its objective was to be the capture of Caen which, it was hoped, would take place that evening, as well as linking up with the 6th Airborne Division. The 3rd Division hit the beach at 07.30 between Lion-sur-Mer and Ouistreham/Riva-Bella. Actually securing the beach cost 630 men killed or wounded. Hermanville was reached relatively quickly as were Périers, Beuville, Biéville and Blainville. The division had just come within sight of Caen at Carpiquet when it was halted by the 21st Panzer Division and driven back to Biéville. From July 18, it took part in Operation 'Goodwood,' a grand design to take Caen, and distinguished itself at Touffréville and, afterwards, at Falaise. The 50th (Northumbrian) Division landed on Gold Beach on June 6, and lost 413 men before the beach was cleared. Its troops then pushed on to take the Mont Fleury battery before liberating Bayeux the following day. In the following weeks, after fighting around Caen, the division held a line from Livry to Lingèvres,

B ayonets fixed, these Scotsmen of the 15th Division await the signal to attack on June 26, 1944. (IWM)

T he PIAT grenade launcher was the standard anti-tank weapon issued to infantry battalions. It appeared in 1942 and could fire a projectile capable of penetrating the armor of all tanks in service at that time. (Militaria Magazine)

Infantrymen of the 3rd Division in July 1944 on the eve of Operation 'Goodwood.' The officers were to suffer the most in Normandy, nearly 30% of battalion, company of platoon officers becoming casualties. (IWM)

Inset: a Mk III helmet bearing the flash of the Royal Welch Fusiliers (53rd Division). Production of this new helmet was begun in November 1943. (IWM)

Tilly and Saint-Pierre until July 8. It then took part in Operation 'Bluecoat' in early August and fought hard for Mont Pinçon close to Falaise and in the Condé-sur-Noireau sector.

The other British formations included the 51st (Highland) division, which landed on June 7, and was engaged at Bourguébus and Falaise; the 49th (West Riding) which landed on June 12 and distinguished itself along the Odon. The 15th (Scottish) landed on the June 14 and reached the front lines on the Odon on the 25th before taking part in the battle for Caen in July and in the struggle for Mont Pinçon in early August. The 43rd (Wessex) arrived in Normandy on June 24 and fought on the Odon, at Caen, at Bourguébus and Mont Pinçon; the 53rd (Welch) landed on June 27 and fought along the Odon, at Mont Pinçon and Falaise. The 59th (Staffordshire) also landed on June 27 and fought at Caen and Mont Pinçon but was later disbanded to provide infantry replacements.

An infantryman ready for battle. He wears the universal-issue Battledress and webbing equipment with ammo pouches on the chest.
(Reconstruction by J. Bouchery/Militaria Magazine)

THE BRITISH GUNNER

British artillery in Normandy consisted of five regiments of superheavy artillery, five of heavy, 21 of medium and seven of field artillery as well as five groups of reserve artillery.

It was an impressive force and one which contributed significantly to the German defeat.

Artillery was organized according to caliber and function. The 25-pdrs were used by the field artillery, 4.5-inch or 5.5-inch guns by the medium artillery, 7.2-inch howitzers and American M1 A1 howitzers by the heavy artillery and 8-inch or American M1 guns by the superheavy artillery.

On D-day only self-propelled guns were landed in the first eight hours.

A 4.5 inch gun in Normandy. This was usually found in Medium regiments of the Army Group Royal Artillery (AGRA) (IWM)

This gunner wears a poncho-groundsheet to protect himself from the rain. Of all Allied combat troops in Normandy, most were gunners (18%), whilst 14% were infantrymen and 13% engineers. (Reconstruction by Militaria Magazine)

*G*unners in action near Caen in July 1944. They are firing the standard 25-pdr field gun-howitzer. In 1944 a towed-battery consisted of 198 men of whom 10 were officers.
(IWM)

*A*n American 155-mm M1 A1 gun in battery. Once the battery was in position all the unit's vehicles were taken to the rear except for those carrying ammunition.
(IWM)

Royal Marine artillery regiments made use of 95-mm close-support tanks on the beaches.

An infantry division had three groups of organic artillery and an armored division just two (one of which usually consisted of self-propelled Sexton 25-pdr or Priests 105-mm howitzers). Front-line divisions usually received support from four field regiments and two medium regiments from army and corps reserve, totaling 128 guns.

British artillery was very mobile and flexible. For the British it was more important to bring pieces into action, neglecting initial adjustments, than to ensure their accuracy (rapid fire raised morale among friendly forces).

The British also preferred to concentrate their fire on zones. The excellent and versatile 25-pdr (from the weight of the projectile) cannon-howitzer, probably the best weapon fielded by the British, helped greatly.

It had such a steady rate of fire that most Germans believed it was an automatic.

*S*tripes as worn by Royal Artillery sergeants.
(Militaria Magazine)

*T*he anti-tank gunners' skill-at-arms badge.
(Militaria Magazine)

THE CANADIAN ARTILLERY OFFICER

Canadian artillery organization was very similar to that used by the British. There was divisional artillery and artillery belonging to the general reserve, the latter normally grouped into two AGRAs (Army Group, Royal Artillery).

This artillery officer wears the khaki beret with flaming-grenade artillery badge.
(Canadian Army Overseas Photo)

The artillery badge worn on peaked caps and side caps.
(Militaria Magazine)

Top: A Smith & Wesson K 38/200 caliber 9-mm revolver, a favorite handgun among officers and tank crews.
(Militaria Magazine)

The Royal Canadian Artillery fielded regiments characterized by specific purpose (field artillery, anti-tank artillery, anti-aircraft artillery and observers) or by type of gun (light, medium or heavy). Each division had three regiments of field artillery (towed 25-pdrs), an anti-tank regiment (towed 17-pdrs) or self-propelled guns, and an anti-aircraft regiment.

During an offensive, the artillery would prepare and support the attack as well as cover the troops until their objective was reached. Preparation meant hitting enemy tanks and artillery or dispersing infantry with salvoes. Then, when the attack was launched, artillery would have to fire in support, setting a barrage down in front of the advancing troops to minimize losses.

Protective fire, which involved firing on enemy observation posts or suspect positions, would then ensue.

In defensive situations, artillery was required to fire at pre-spotted points as the enemy advanced, bring down massive counter-fire if possible and, finally, stop the enemy's

Formation badge of the 2nd Canadian Corps Artillery
(Militaria Magazine)

Normandy 1944, a self-propelled 105-mm howitzer crew, assigned to the 3rd Canadian infantry division for close support during the D-Day assault.
(Public Archives of Canada)

July 1944: A gun crew cleans the barrel of a 5.5 in. gun of the 1st Canadian Army. (Public Archives of Canada)

advance by firing directly at the head of their column.

The coordination of battery fire, or the bringing together of massive concentrations of fire, was made much easier by radio communication as this allowed observers, batteries and liaison teams assigned to infantry or armored units to work together. Observation teams on the ground were complemented by aerial observation from light aircraft.

Top: large map case used by artillery observers or reconnaissance units.
(Militaria Magazine)

This Canadian officer wears field dress with standard web equipment. He has a holster for his No 2 Mk I Smith & Wesson revolver, a binocular case, a cartridge case and a compass case on the belt.
(Reconstruction by Militaria Magazine)

THE RADIO OPERATOR

Wireless communications played a crucial part in the course of the campaign and British officers were able to call up artillery support, aerial assistance, reinforcements or establish the position of neighboring units all by means of radio.

The Royal Corps of Signals had units present at all levels of command. They were represented at Army and Army Group level, at Army Corps level (with a HQ and three companies) and at divisional

Infantry signalers of the 50th Division in June 1944, using a No 18 Wireless set. This had a maximum range of 12 miles. The No 18 set was used for company-to-battalion communication. British Army sets were not as efficient or dependable as contemporary state-of-the-art American radios. (IWM)

Insignia worn by a radio wireless operator attached to an infantry division. (Militaria Magazine)

level. Radio signalers working with infantry divisions ensured communications were maintained at all levels or with neighboring divisions. Signals units attached to a division consisted of a staff, a HQ company and four companies for exploitation and construction, the latter divided into specific roles: radio, wire, liaison and operations.

Signals units attached to armored divisions were usually well equipped and enjoyed a vast number of radio sets (more than 500). Some British infantry sections

Top: Signalmen at the front. (Militaria Magazine)

A British field telephone set Mark 5. (Militaria Magazine)

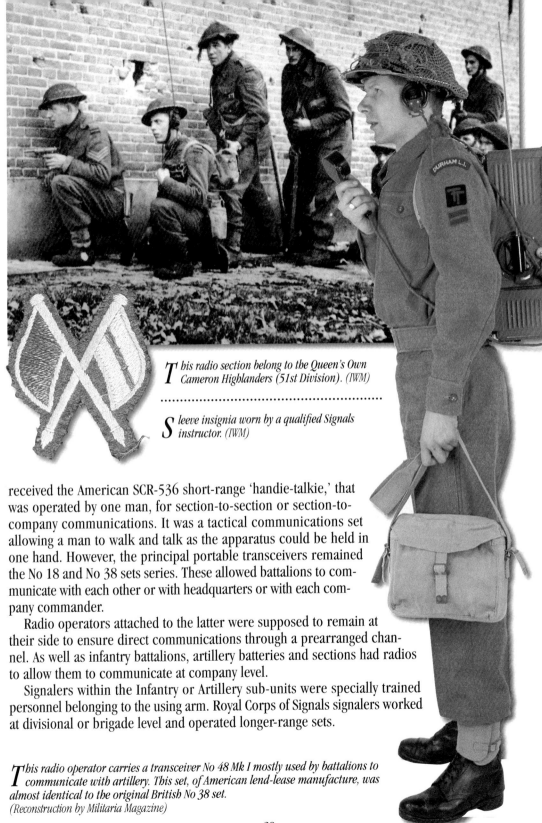

*T his radio section belong to the Queen's Own
Cameron Highlanders (51st Division). (IWM)*

···

*S leeve insignia worn by a qualified Signals
instructor. (IWM)*

received the American SCR-536 short-range 'handie-talkie,' that
was operated by one man, for section-to-section or section-to-
company communications. It was a tactical communications set
allowing a man to walk and talk as the apparatus could be held in
one hand. However, the principal portable transceivers remained
the No 18 and No 38 sets series. These allowed battalions to communicate with each other or with headquarters or with each company commander.

Radio operators attached to the latter were supposed to remain at
their side to ensure direct communications through a prearranged channel. As well as infantry battalions, artillery batteries and sections had radios
to allow them to communicate at company level.

Signalers within the Infantry or Artillery sub-units were specially trained
personnel belonging to the using arm. Royal Corps of Signals signalers worked
at divisional or brigade level and operated longer-range sets.

*T his radio operator carries a transceiver No 48 Mk I mostly used by battalions to
communicate with artillery. This set, of American lend-lease manufacture, was
almost identical to the original British No 38 set.*
(Reconstruction by Militaria Magazine)

THE MILITARY POLICEMAN

Organized into companies or sections, military policemen were present among all army formations and in the rear areas.

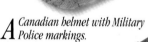

*O*n the road from Caen to Falaise, in August 1944. Two corporals belonging to the 2nd Canadian Provost Company put up road signs.
(Public Archives of Canada)

A Canadian helmet with Military Police markings.
(J. Bouchery collection)

Their main tasks involved the marking out of routes (with signs and placards), the regulation of traffic and vehicles, guarding and transferring prisoners of war and the control of civilians in the operational zone, the overseeing of military dress and procedure whilst troops were in garrison or on leave. Another branch of service, the Military Provost Staff

A bove: Two Canadian MP corporals on motorbikes. They wear the fiber crash helmet. The 'C' prefix to the registration number on the fuel tank indicates a Canadian army vehicle.
(Public Archives of Canada)

T he Sten 9-mm submachine-gun was standard issue to MPs in the field.
(Militaria Magazine)

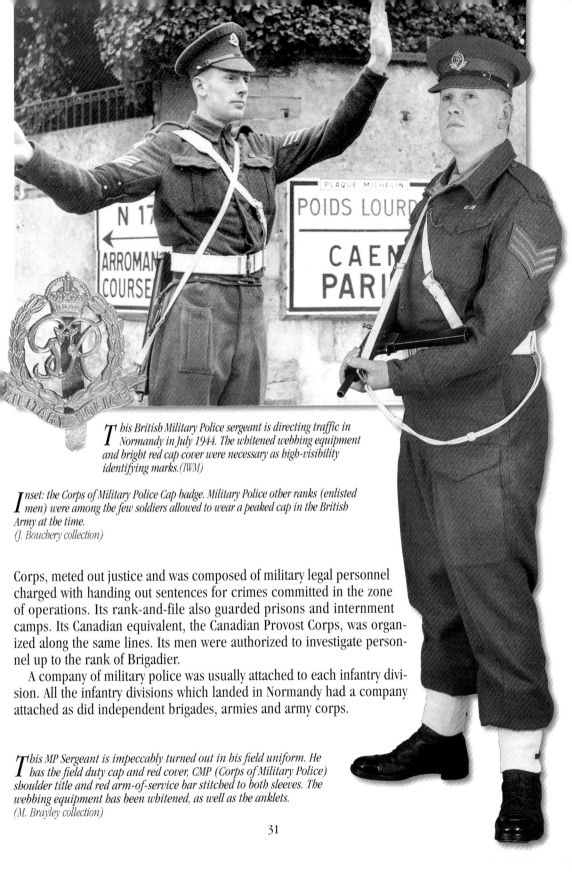

*T*his British Military Police sergeant is directing traffic in
Normandy in July 1944. The whitened webbing equipment
and bright red cap cover were necessary as high-visibility
identifying marks.(IWM)

*I*nset: the Corps of Military Police Cap badge. Military Police other ranks (enlisted
men) were among the few soldiers allowed to wear a peaked cap in the British
Army at the time.
(J. Bouchery collection)

Corps, meted out justice and was composed of military legal personnel
charged with handing out sentences for crimes committed in the zone
of operations. Its rank-and-file also guarded prisons and internment
camps. Its Canadian equivalent, the Canadian Provost Corps, was organized along the same lines. Its men were authorized to investigate personnel up to the rank of Brigadier.

A company of military police was usually attached to each infantry division. All the infantry divisions which landed in Normandy had a company
attached as did independent brigades, armies and army corps.

*T*his MP Sergeant is impeccably turned out in his field uniform. He
has the field duty cap and red cover, CMP (Corps of Military Police)
shoulder title and red arm-of-service bar stitched to both sleeves. The
webbing equipment has been whitened, as well as the anklets.
(M. Brayley collection)

THE MEDICAL ORDERLY

*The medical corps' primary tasks were
to keep units up to strength, prepare
and enforce hygiene in the field, tend
the sick and care for or evacuate the wounded.*

The British knew that they were deploying 800,000 men for the invasion and prepared to deal with an estimated casualty figure of at least 22,500. For this they mobilized 190 medical units of all kinds and made 40,000 hospital beds available (including Canadian facilities). Unfortunately, the demands of the Italian and Middle Eastern fronts meant that there was a real lack of experienced medical personnel for the Normandy invasion. At dawn on June 6, 1,154 members of the Royal Army Medical Corps landed with the 3rd Division. The 225th Field Ambulance company was dropped with the 6th Airborne Division at 01.00 on June 6. Everything went well and by 03.30 it had established a first aid post.

In combatant units, casualties were tended to by medical personnel attached to each battalion and its subunits, who administered first-aid on the battlefield. These were usually stretchered off afterwards to battalion first aid posts. The casualty was then evacuated on foot or by ambulance, depending upon the nature of his wound, to a field hospital. From there he was sent to a surgical unit or, if ambulatory, directed to a rear-area hospital.

*C*rushable chloroform
ampules and disposable dose
of morphine.
(Militaria Magazine)

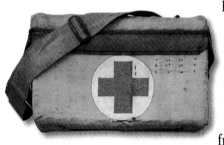

A wicker and canvas field first
aid kit. It contains dressings,
bandages, antiseptics and
evacuation tags.
(Militaria Magazine)

*B*ellow: An evacuation tag.
This was tied to wounded or
dead. Evacuation of the severely
wounded from Normandy was
carried out by special ships or by
planes flying from four airstrips
reserved for this task.
(Militaria Magazine)

*T*op: July 1944, a stretcher bearer of the Royal Welch
Fusiliers (53rd Division) prepares supplies to
replenish his field kit. Probably a bandsman or
member of the battalion's administrative platoon,
he has been trained in emergency medical measures.
His task is first-aid and early evacuation to the Regimental
Aid Post (RAP) (IWM)

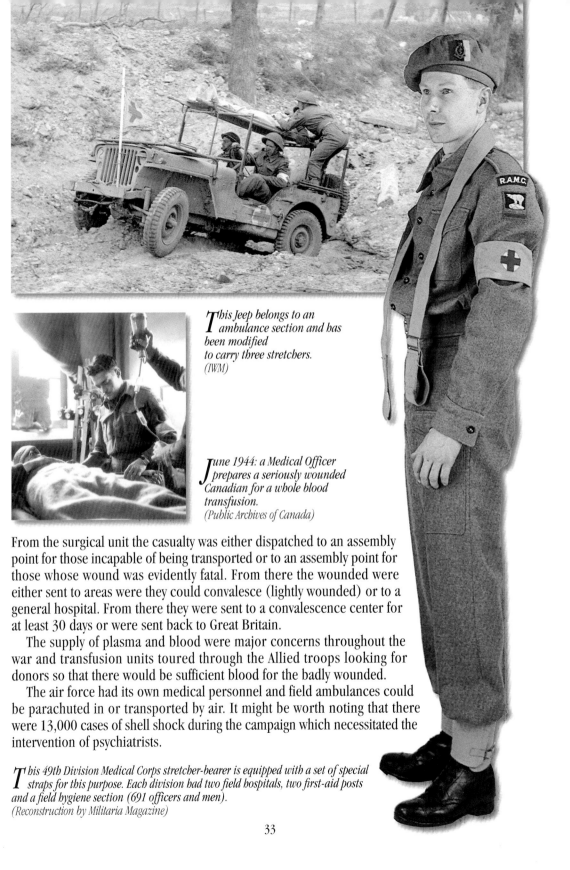

This Jeep belongs to an ambulance section and has been modified to carry three stretchers.
(IWM)

June 1944: a Medical Officer prepares a seriously wounded Canadian for a whole blood transfusion.
(Public Archives of Canada)

From the surgical unit the casualty was either dispatched to an assembly point for those incapable of being transported or to an assembly point for those whose wound was evidently fatal. From there the wounded were either sent to areas were they could convalesce (lightly wounded) or to a general hospital. From there they were sent to a convalescence center for at least 30 days or were sent back to Great Britain.

The supply of plasma and blood were major concerns throughout the war and transfusion units toured through the Allied troops looking for donors so that there would be sufficient blood for the badly wounded.

The air force had its own medical personnel and field ambulances could be parachuted in or transported by air. It might be worth noting that there were 13,000 cases of shell shock during the campaign which necessitated the intervention of psychiatrists.

This 49th Division Medical Corps stretcher-bearer is equipped with a set of special straps for this purpose. Each division had two field hospitals, two first-aid posts and a field hygiene section (691 officers and men).
(Reconstruction by Militaria Magazine)

PRACTICAL INFORMATION

In this section we have provided practical guidance on sites and museums of interest in Normandy. We have included details of the most representative sites and those located as close as possible to the actual events covered in this book. Military vehicle enthusiasts are referred to the practical information sections of our 'Armor in Normandy' guides.

In CALVADOS

Five miles to the north of Caen, at Ouistreham, is a **museum commemorating the landing of the British No. 4 Commando**. Uniforms, weapons and equipment are on display as well as documents relating to the landing of British and Free French commandos at Sword Beach. The site is dedicated to the 177 French commandos. There's also a monument alongside the D514 road, as it enters the south of the town, and another on the sea front.

Musée du débarquement des commandos No 4
Place Alfred-Thomas
14150 Ouistreham
Tel: 02 31 96 63 10

Further along the coast, 15 miles to the east, near Benerville-sur-Mer, is **Mont Canisy**, transformed by the Germans into one of the largest coastal batteries of the Atlantic Wall. There are numerous casemates, bunkers, observation posts and gun positions to visit, as well as 20 miles of tunnels.

Site de la batterie du Belvedere au Mont Canisy
Les Amis du Mont Canisy
Mairie
14910 Benerville-sur-Mer
Tel: 02 31 87 92 64
Fax: 02 31 87 32 15

Opening hours: April to September, Saturday and Sunday 14.30 to 17.30.

There are free guided tours which last 2 hours. These are given by local enthusiasts of the site preservation society. There is car parking.
Bring torches.

Turning back towards Bayeux, the **Memorial museum to General de Gaulle** recalls the great man's visit to the city on June 14, 1944 and June 16, 1946. There are numerous photos and documents on display and films are also shown.

General de Gaulle Memorial Museum
10 rue Bourbesneur
14400 Bayeux
Tel: 02 31 92 45 55
Opening hours: 15 March to 15 November, 09.30 to 12.30 and 14.00 to 18.30.

The largest British War cemetery of World War II is to the south of Bayeux. It contains the graves of 4,648 Allied and German soldiers, of which 3,935 are British. Heading west along Route Nationale 13, the visitor will reach the vast **La Cambe cemetery**. Here 21,500 German soldiers lie buried beneath five huge black crosses. There is a memorial chapel at the entrance. Another **German cemetery** lies close by at Saint-Germain-du-Pert.

Five miles from there, on the coast, is the **Rangers Museum** at Grandcamp Maisy. It commemorates this elite American unit and its attack on Pointe du Hoc on D-Day.

Rangers Museum
Mairie (town hall)
14450 Grandcamp-Maisy
Tel: 02 31 92 33 51

Heading along the D514 you reach Vierville-sur-Mer and the **Omaha beach museum**: an impressive collection of equipment, uniforms, artillery, weapons and even aircraft engines.

Musée D-day d'Omaha
Route de Grandcamp
14710 Vierville-sur-Mer
Tel: 02 31 21 71 80
Open 30 March to 10 November.

Some three miles further down the D514 is Colleville-sur-Mer with its **American Cemetery**. It covers 20 hectares and there are more than 9,000 white crosses. Most of the soldiers buried here were killed during the landing. There is a memorial chapel to American youth.

Further inland, some twenty miles to the south west of Bayeux is a memorial museum dedicated to the fighting in bocage country.

Musée de la Percée du Bocage
14350 Saint-Martin-des-Besaces
Tel: 02 31 67 52 78

The **Friends of the Suffolk Regiment** organize visits and guided tours of the Hillman fortifications at Colleville-Montgomery, a German command post with 18 emplacements which was taken by the 1st battalion of the regiment on June 7, 1944.

Friends of the Suffolk Regiment
Mairie de Colleville-Montgomery
Tel: 02 31 97 12 61
www.amis-du-suffolk-rgt.com
Open every Tuesday until 15.00 in July and August. Tours last 1.30 hours.

IN THE MANCHE REGION

Crossing into the Manche region on the Route Nationale (RN) 13 one soon reaches the Carentan canal and then Sainte-Marie-du-Mont with its **Utah Beach museum**. It is the only museum dedicated to the landings there in the entire region and the exhibits are first class. Allied assault equipment and German defensive equipment are presented and videos are shown in three languages. There's a panoramic view over Utah Beach itself and Pointe-du-Hoc.

Utah Beach Museum
50480 Sainte-Marie-du-Mont
Tel: 02 33 71 53 35

Opening hours: 15 March to 15 November, 10.00 to 12.30 and 14.00 to 17.30.

Another fascinating site is 10 miles to the north-west at Crisbecq. It's the **Battery of Azeville and Saint-Marcouf**. There were four casemates here, armed with 105 mm guns and eight blockhouses with a garrison of 170 artillerymen. There is also a flak position, underground bunkers and stores.